HALLUCINOGENS
AFFECTING LIVES

BY ASHLEY STORM

MOMENTUM

The Child's World®
childsworld.com

Published by The Child's World®
1980 Lookout Drive • Mankato, MN 56003-1705
800-599-READ • www.childsworld.com

Photographs ©: Shutterstock Images, cover,
12, 16, 18, 22; Red Line Editorial, 5; Yuliia
Hurzhos/Shutterstock Images, 6; Light Field
Studios/Shutterstock Images, 8, 10, 24;
Photographee.eu/Shutterstock Images, 11; Impact
Photography/Shutterstock Images, 14; PR Image
Factory/Shutterstock Images, 15; Charles Russell/
Shutterstock Images, 20; Yakobchuk Viacheslav/
Shutterstock Images, 26; iStockphoto, 28

ISBN 9781503844933 (Reinforced Library Binding)
ISBN 9781503846418 (Portable Document Format)
ISBN 9781503847606 (Online Multi-user eBook)
LCCN 2019957753

Printed in the United States of America

Some names and details have been changed
throughout this book to protect privacy.

CONTENTS

MOMENTUM

FAST FACTS

What They Are

▶ Hallucinogens are drugs that make a person see, hear, or feel things that aren't really there. These effects are called hallucinations.

▶ Some hallucinogens come from plants or mushrooms. Others are made in laboratories.

▶ Examples of hallucinogens include LSD, PCP, psilocybin (sy-luh-SY-ben)—or "magic mushrooms"—and peyote, which can come from cacti or be made in labs.

▶ MDMA, also called "molly" or "ecstasy," is not classified as a hallucinogen. However, MDMA can have mind-altering effects that are similar to hallucinogens.

How They're Used

▶ Hallucinogens are most commonly smoked or eaten. A hallucinogen can also be melted on the tongue when it is in the form of a small, square piece of paper.

Physical Effects

▶ A person's body temperature, heart rate, and blood pressure may increase.

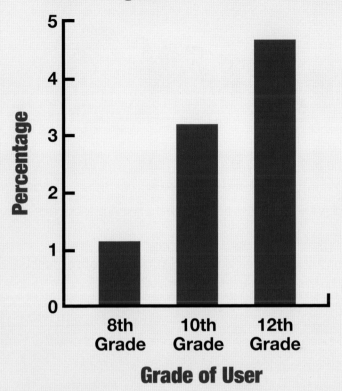

Hallucinogen Use in the Past Year

Percentage (y-axis: 0, 1, 2, 3, 4, 5)

Grade of User (x-axis: 8th Grade, 10th Grade, 12th Grade)

"Hallucinogens." *National Institute on Drug Abuse*, n.d., drugabuse.gov. Accessed 29 Jan. 2020.

In a 2019 national survey, researchers found that within the past year, it was more common for older teenagers to have used hallucinogens than it was for younger teenagers to have used the drugs.

▶ People may experience **withdrawal** symptoms when they stop using hallucinogens.

Mental Effects

▶ A person may experience hallucinations, **paranoia**, and changes in personality.

CHAPTER ONE

VIOLENT BEHAVIOR

O n a beautiful day in October, Joshua hiked with his best friend in Rocky Mountain National Park. Joshua and Jack loved to walk the trails along the river in the fall. Joshua liked the gold, red, and orange leaves that surrounded them. The day was warm and sunny, and he could see snow on the mountaintops in the distance.

Joshua looked through his binoculars. He scanned the mountains until he saw an elk in the valley below them. It was an animal with big antlers. Joshua turned to tell his friend, but Jack was staring into space. Jack looked dizzy, like he might fall over. Joshua sighed and jammed his binoculars into his backpack. He could tell that his friend had used LSD, even though Joshua had asked him not to. Jack had been using LSD a lot lately. Why couldn't Jack just enjoy being in the mountains like he used to?

◄ **When someone is using hallucinogens, he or she might space out and be unaware of his or her surroundings.**

Before Jack started using drugs, he would have been excited to see an elk in the park. Now, he didn't seem to care about anything at all. Joshua missed how his friend used to be.

Joshua hiked the rest of the trail quickly, with Jack trailing a few feet behind. When they reached the end of the trail, they walked back to Joshua's car. Jack had been very quiet, but Joshua was annoyed with his friend and didn't want to talk anyway. They put on their seatbelts, and Joshua eased the car onto the road.

They hadn't driven far when Jack suddenly pounded his fist into the dashboard. He screamed for no reason. Joshua pulled the car to the side of the road. He tried to calm Jack down, but it was no use. Jack was hallucinating. He was yelling and punching at things that weren't there. He didn't even seem to know who Joshua was. Joshua didn't want to leave his friend, but it wasn't safe to stay in the car. He took his keys, reached for the door handle, and got out.

Joshua stood beside the car for a few minutes, hoping that his friend would calm down. But Jack continued to yell loudly and throw punches at the air. Joshua used his phone to call for help. He sat on the side of the road to wait for park rangers to arrive. He could still hear Jack screaming in the car.

◀ **LSD can cause people to become violent.**

▲ **LSD is an illegal substance. Someone who possesses or uses the drug could get arrested.**

The park rangers arrived quickly, but Joshua felt like hours had passed. The sun was starting to set. His friend hadn't stopped yelling the whole time. Joshua explained the situation to the rangers. It took two rangers to get ahold of Jack. Joshua watched helplessly as they put handcuffs around Jack's wrists.

As the rangers drove away with Jack in their back seat, Joshua felt terrible. He just had his friend arrested. But what else could Joshua do? He opened the car door and saw that his rearview mirror was busted. Jack must have broken it.

▲ Rehabilitation programs offer help to those who struggle with drug abuse.

Joshua didn't leave right away. He pulled out his phone and did some research about LSD. He learned that the drug could make people violent. If Jack continued using LSD, it could even change his personality. Joshua feared for his friend's health. As the sun dipped below the mountain, Joshua thought of all the times he and Jack had hiked and of all the sunsets they had seen. Joshua started to research how he could help his friend. He found websites for **rehabilitation** (rehab) programs in the area. Joshua wasn't sure what would be the best fit for Jack, but he knew one thing for certain. He was not going to give up on his friend.

CHAPTER TWO

WHAT IS REAL?

Adam gripped the leather football and focused on the goal line further down the beach. He blocked out the noise of crashing waves, laughing children, and music blaring from a nearby speaker. Nothing would distract Adam from getting to that goal line. Out of the corner of his eye, he saw his older brother running toward him. Jared was fast, but Adam pushed his legs to move faster. As Adam leaped across the goal line, Jared tackled him. They crashed to the ground. Most of Jared's weight landed on Adam's leg. Adam's ankle exploded in pain.

At the hospital, the doctor told Adam he had broken his ankle. The doctor gave Adam medication for the pain. Adam liked the way the **prescription** drugs made him feel. He became calm and relaxed when he took them.

◄ **A doctor might give painkillers to someone who gets injured.**

▲ **LSD might come in the form of a small piece of paper that dissolves on the tongue.**

One night, Adam went to a party at a friend's house. His friends began a game of football in the backyard. Adam couldn't play. He had been stuck in an ankle cast for two weeks. He wouldn't be able to play sports for at least six more weeks. Adam would give anything to play football again. Feeling sad, he went inside the house to be alone. But the house wasn't empty.

▲ **LSD often makes people experience sights and sounds that are not real. These hallucinations can be scary.**

There were people sitting in a circle on the floor in the living room. They laughed and stared off into space. Adam realized they were using drugs. They asked Adam if he wanted to try LSD. Adam wondered if LSD would give him the same carefree feeling as his prescription medicine. Everyone seemed like they were having fun. Adam wanted to have fun, too. He nodded, and they gave him a tiny, square piece of paper. They told Adam to put it on his tongue. The paper melted when he put it there.

▲ **Someone going through withdrawal might become anxious and have trouble concentrating.**

Adam quickly realized the LSD didn't feel like his pain medicine. Everything looked and sounded strange. The furniture seemed to move by itself. It looked like the color of the walls brightened, and people's voices seemed louder. He thought it was funny.

Adam started to hang out with the teens who gave him the LSD. They used LSD a lot. Adam **craved** the imaginary world he entered into when he took the drug. He liked the way it made him feel smarter, like a superhuman. He wanted to use it every day. He stopped spending time with his other friends. He didn't even spend much time with his brother.

When Adam's cast was finally removed, his brother asked if he wanted to play football. Adam said he had plans with his other friends. His brother was confused. Since when did Adam not want to play football? Jared told him that he missed hanging out together. Adam realized he felt the same way. Adam was wasting all of his time on LSD, which made him experience things that weren't real, such as seeing colorful patterns and smelling sounds. Adam decided to try to stop using the drug.

Adam wasn't physically **addicted** to LSD, but mentally he craved it. Adam soon grew anxious. He couldn't concentrate in school, and he kept experiencing flashbacks to the times he took LSD. Adam was going through withdrawal. He wished he could just take more of the drug and return to his imaginary world. Scared he would take more LSD, Adam told Jared how he was feeling. His brother and parents encouraged Adam to see a therapist. With a therapist's help, and with his family's support, Adam eventually stopped craving LSD as much.

CHAPTER THREE

EARNING TRUST

Connor listened to the beeping of the machines. He was in a hospital bed. Tubes and wires connected him to the machines to monitor his heartbeat. Connor had gotten into a fight with a drug dealer, who was someone he gave money to in exchange for drugs. He knew his broken bones should heal in six weeks. The doctors had said Connor would be able to leave the hospital in just a couple of days. But Connor didn't know where he would go. He felt tears pool in his eyes. His parents never came to visit him in the hospital. He had lied to them too many times, and now his parents couldn't trust him.

It had only been a few days since Connor's parents kicked him out of the house. His parents had tried to make him follow their rules. They said Connor had to get a job and learn responsibility. They even gave him a curfew. He ignored them.

◀ **Drug deals are dangerous and illegal.**

▲ **People who smoke a lot of PCP build up a tolerance to it.**

Connor was 18 years old and thought he could do whatever he wanted. So, Connor's parents told him he couldn't live with them anymore. They said they needed to focus on his younger brothers and sisters.

As Connor lay in his hospital bed, he thought about what had led him to this point. He came from a large family. He didn't fit in with his brothers and sisters. He felt like an outsider. When he was younger, he started hanging out with troublemakers. His friends introduced him to drugs. By the time Connor turned 16, he was addicted to PCP. Connor smoked PCP every day. Soon, he needed to smoke larger amounts to feel its effects. This is because Connor had developed a **tolerance**.

His PCP use soon became expensive. Connor began to steal things to pay for the drug. He took money from his parents. He stole birthday money from his little brothers and sisters. He even stole from the neighbors. Connor developed a bad reputation in the neighborhood. Whenever something went missing, the neighbors blamed Connor.

Connor's parents tried to help him. They hired lawyers and got him out of jail a few times. They took him to **counselors**. They spent so much money trying to help Connor with his addiction that there wasn't much money left over for the things his brothers and sisters wanted. They didn't get to take piano or dance classes. The family didn't have money for vacations. Connor's siblings grew angry with him.

Nothing seemed to help Connor. He continued to use PCP. His personality changed. He became mean to his family and said hateful things. His parents didn't trust him with his younger siblings. They were afraid he might hurt them.

Eventually, Connor started selling drugs. It was dangerous, but he didn't care. He needed the money to buy more PCP. Nothing else mattered. Then, he ended up alone in a hospital bed.

The day Connor was released from the hospital, he couldn't stop crying. He was scared and lonely. He knew he had to change his life. A nurse helped him find a rehabilitation center.

▲ **Some rehab centers help people become independent by finding jobs and places to live.**

When Connor's parents tried to get him help, he hadn't taken it seriously. This time he did.

It wasn't easy. PCP is very addictive, and Connor had been using it for many years. The withdrawal symptoms were terrible. Connor's body had to adjust to no longer having the drug.

He also had severe anxiety. For months, Connor had to fight the temptation to use PCP again, but he stayed strong. As part of his rehab, workers at the program helped him find a job and an apartment. For the first time in years, Connor was hopeful for the future. He still had a lot of work to do to fix his relationship with his family, though. It would be hard to earn back their trust. But Connor was determined to try.

GETTING HELP

If someone is worried about a friend, or if he or she is struggling with addiction themselves, they can talk to a teacher or a school counselor. A person also can reach out to a support group, such as Nar-Anon, an organization for people with loved ones who are living with addiction. The Substance Abuse and Mental Health Services Administration has information about support groups and rehab programs. For more information, visit SAMHSA.org or call their hotline at 1-800-662-HELP.

CHAPTER FOUR

YOUR HONOR

Trina wiped her sweaty palms on her dark jeans as she stood at the front of the courtroom. She felt small with the judge looking down at her from the bench. Trina was glad to have her lawyer standing beside her. She felt stronger with the lawyer by her side. Trina hoped he could help her so she wouldn't have to go to prison for a long time. Trina had been arrested. A police officer had caught her selling PCP and brought Trina to jail.

As the judge read through some notes, Trina's thoughts drifted to what had brought her here. She used PCP every day. The PCP had caused her to do a lot of things that she regretted. One time, she took off her jacket when it was below freezing outside, and she got frostbite. Trina hadn't been thinking clearly. The PCP made her feel like her skin was on fire.

◄ **People who get caught dealing drugs could go to prison for a long time.**

▲ **PCP has physical effects on the body. It might raise someone's body temperature so she or he feels very warm.**

Trina had dropped out of high school because of her addiction. At school, she couldn't smoke PCP, and that's all she wanted to do. She worked customer service jobs for a while, but she only cared about getting **high**. Trina became a drug dealer. That's when she got caught for selling PCP.

Now, Trina stood in court and hoped she wouldn't have to go to prison. Her lawyer said if she admitted guilt, he would be able to convince the judge to reduce her prison time. Trina agreed to plead guilty.

Trina's lawyer was able to help her. Because Trina was 19 and had never been in serious trouble, the judge said she could join a drug court program instead of going to prison. Trina would have to go to rehab while someone from the court checked up on her. If Trina completed drug court, her record would be wiped clean. It would be like she had never gotten into trouble. But if she used drugs again, she would have to go to prison for five years.

PRISON SENTENCING

The United States has the highest imprisonment rate in the world. There are around 2.3 million people in prison in the United States. A lot of these people are serving time for drug-related crimes. Almost half of the people in federal prisons are there for a drug offense. Many judges believe prison is not necessary for people addicted to drugs. Instead, they may send people to a rehabilitation program or drug court, which specializes in drug-related cases.

▲ **Drug courts decide whether someone who uses drugs should go to prison or get treatment.**

Trina was worried. For 18 months, she would have to follow all the rules of drug court. She had to go to meetings. She was required to have a job. She wasn't allowed to use drugs or alcohol. That scared Trina. Could she stop using PCP?

First, Trina went to drug rehabilitation to help her safely stop using PCP. After that, she got a job at a grocery store. The PCP use still had some long-term effects on her brain, though. It was hard for Trina to focus. Sometimes, she had trouble remembering.

After a few months, she started to think more clearly. Trina thought about going to college. First, she would need to graduate high school online.

It was hard, but Trina finished drug court. There was a ceremony. Trina's lawyer came. Trina told him that she had graduated high school and was going to go to college. He asked Trina what she wanted to study. Trina smiled at him. She told him she wanted to be a lawyer.

THINK ABOUT IT

▶ In your opinion, what are the worst things that drug addiction can do to a person?

▶ Do you think court-ordered drug rehabilitation is a good idea? Or should people not be forced to get treatment against their will?

▶ Why would someone try hallucinogens if they are dangerous?

GLOSSARY

addicted (uh-DIK-tid): Someone who is addicted feels a very strong need to do or have something regularly. People who use hallucinogens can become addicted to the drugs.

counselors (KOWN-suh-lurs): Counselors are people who offer advice. Many people with addictions visit counselors for help handling their addiction.

craved (KRAYVD): A person who craved something had uncontrollable desires to have it. When Adam stopped using LSD, he craved it.

high (HYE): Being high on a drug means having the feeling of euphoria from taking the drug. Many people use hallucinogens to get high.

paranoia (payr-uh-NOY-uh): Paranoia is being extremely suspicious without reason. Someone who takes a hallucinogen may experience paranoia.

prescription (pri-SKRIP-shun): A prescription is a doctor's written note that allows a patient to receive a given treatment. Some people misuse prescription medication.

rehabilitation (ree-uh-bil-uh-TAY-shun): Drug rehabilitation is a type of treatment for drug abuse. Most rehabilitation centers have strict rules for patients.

tolerance (TOL-ur-uhnss): Someone who takes a lot of drugs builds up a tolerance and has to take more to feel their effects. The man had a high tolerance, so he had to smoke more hallucinogens to get high.

withdrawal (with-DRAW-uhl): Withdrawal is the experience of physical and mental effects when a person stops taking an addictive drug. Withdrawal makes it hard for people to quit using hallucinogens.

BOOKS

Petersen, Christine. *Ecstasy*. New York, NY: Marshall Cavendish, 2014.

Scott, Celicia. *Hard Drugs: Cocaine, LSD, PCP, & Heroin*. Broomall, PA: Mason Crest, 2015.

Sheff, David. *High: Everything You Want to Know about Drugs, Alcohol, and Addiction*. Boston, MA: Houghton Mifflin Harcourt, 2018.

WEBSITES

Visit our website for links about addiction to hallucinogens: **childsworld.com/links**

Note to Parents, Teachers, and Librarians: We routinely verify our Web links to make sure they are safe and active sites. So encourage your readers to check them out!

SELECTED BIBLIOGRAPHY

"Hallucinogens." *National Institute on Drug Abuse*, n.d., drugabuse.gov. Accessed 29 Jan. 2020.

"How Can I Tell If Someone Is Using Drugs?" *Positive Choices*, 8 Nov. 2019, positivechoices.org. Accessed 29 Jan. 2020.

Sawyer, Wendy and Peter Wagner. "Mass Incarceration: The Whole Pie 2019." *Prison Policy Initiative*, 19 March 2019, prisonpolicy.org. Accessed 29 Jan. 2020.

INDEX

ABOUT THE AUTHOR

Ashley Storm lives in Kentucky with her husband, three mischievous cats, and a flock of chickens who peck on the back door to demand treats. She enjoys writing for kids of all ages. When she's not writing, she usually has her nose stuck in a book.